In and Out
of the Darkness

Kathleen Koch

DORRANCE
PUBLISHING CO
EST. 1920
PITTSBURGH, PENNSYLVANIA 15238

Dorrance Publishing Co
585 Alpha Drive
Suite 103
Pittsburgh, PA 15238
Visit our website at *www.dorrancebookstore.com*

ISBN: 978-1-6453-0403-6
eISBN: 978-1-6453-0427-2

Power to Believe

Never let go of your dreams
Even though they may seem impossible
When you feel you just can't keep going
You have to always believe in the power of you
Even if you have some struggles and want to gripe
You have to always believe in your precious life
Don't run away without expressing your point of view
Because you need to believe in the power of you

Depression

Depression has a dark side
Sadness that doesn't go away
You try as hard as possible
To make it go away
Trying to not let it bother you
But you don't know how to stop it
These feelings come out of nowhere
And nowhere can happen anywhere
Depression just hits you
It makes you feel like you're in a hole
People don't understand how it may feel
Some thinking it's not real
Being sad and depressed doesn't discriminate
It can happen to anyone
Don't put your feelings on the back burner
You need to set your feelings free

Sorrow

Today sorrow fills the air
Tears falling down people's faces
Saying goodbye to a teenager
Definitely the hardest thing one has to do
Why do some teenagers think they're invincible
Why are drugs so appealing to them
What really makes them even try
They don't think anything will happen to them
Drugs may take over their life
You're always craving more and more
Wondering how am I going to pay for them
Am I going to have enough money for drugs
So I can get through until the next high
Who really wants to go to rehab
Some end up saying, I just can't take these withdrawal symptoms
But I have to try to get myself together
Discharging early because I just can't take it anymore
I really want that first high again
It finally was the last time getting high as a teenager
Because the sunshine turned into darkness
And it ended a young life

How Deep I Feel

Your face is so warm and true
Could you really be real
I just can't imagine
The deepness I feel
When I'm with you
You take away my fears
It all seems so dramatically clear
As we look into each other's eyes
You seem to see right through me
Makes me want to never let you go
I definitely know your above the rest
Both of us being hurt before
I do believe you truly are the best
Nobody understands why I think that
Maybe because I love you the best

Forget His Love

Forget all the nice things he used to do
Forget how much you fell in love with him
Sometimes fun times have got to go
Forget that crazy feeling when you saw him pass by
Forget how many times he made you cry
Forget the voice when he spoke your name
Right now, things just aren't the same
Forget the loving teasing way
Forget you saw him practically everyday
Forget all the things you did together
Because now that girl loves him, too
Forget how many times you were intimate together
Try to remember things are in the past now
Forget he said he wouldn't leave
Forget he said he wouldn't make you cry
Instead he lied and said good bye

Matthew, Zachary, and Gavin

Different days you all came along
Which totally changed my life forever
Being a mother was so much more than I ever thought it would be
The unconditional love you feel for them
Love is different between a mother and son
The ultimate bond which binds you together forever
This will never fade away
It is so unbelievable
How love grows day by day
Stronger and stronger
Where ever you are
Whatever state or country you might be in
Where ever this beautiful life takes you
By land, air, or sea
Your mother I will forever be

Military Boots

What is it like to wear military boots
Boots that travel by air, land, and sea
The sand where they land is quite a site, we will never see
Receiving medals and awards for a job well done
People can't express their gratitude for exactly what you really do
Away from loved ones for months even years at a time
Some people just don't understand when someone is not right there
You feel selfish because you always want them near
The time feels like a lifetime when their away
You pray and pray every night they will call again soon
Or they get their orders to come home soon
Like the day they left to go handle their job
Hopefully when they return home to a screaming mob
Thanking them for a tremendous job

Cupid's Arrow

February is a special month
Hearts and cupid come to mind
Cupid with the golden arrow
Will that golden arrow come my way
Hitting me is always a possibility
Maybe the start of something great
I will want you and need you
And I will never stray without you

Valentine's Day

There is a special day in February
It is meant to bring couples together
Sometimes it's hard to say how and what you feel
I do feel this relationship is extremely real
The love seems mutual from me to you and you to me
I am so glad we have gotten to this point
Valentine's Day is slowly approaching
I really can't wait to see
The love that transpires from you to me

Fighting Depression

Crying and crying and just can't stop
There is nothing you can do
My emotions are as high as can be
Sadness takes over my body
No one seems to understand how this feeling takes over
Feels like someone is squeezing the life out of you
And that feeling just won't let go
Depression is hard to handle all alone
It's bad enough that you feel all alone
You feel like no one can relate
Sometimes you feel like a tiny little mole
Stuck in a deep dark hole
Wanting desperately for someone to help
Help dig me out of this dark hole
But it seems to be that I don't have any help at all

Blanket

How does it feel to be someone's blanket
Being dragged around everywhere
Getting oh so dirty and being washed
It's so exciting being someone's blanket
New adventures, new places, and new people
A child loving you just the way you are
Doesn't matter how fluffy you are
Or that you can't talk back
Someone loves you unconditionally
Someone talks to you all the time
Even when no one else is there
Blanket you give advice
Even though you didn't realize it
Someone relies on you for everything
Even if they forget you on their bed sometimes

Feeling Stupid

Fight and fight
Does it ever stop
Why does it make you feel so stupid
Does it make them feel better
But it doesn't make me feel better
It's the way that you talk to me
I don't think we set out to fight with each other
Your nit-picking way just doesn't seem to end
You make me feel like an idiot
Is this really the objective
Than making it all about you

Something Wrong

Never can you do anything right
Get ignored and people don't want to deal with you
Your feelings just don't go away
Why doesn't anyone ask what's wrong
Why do you feel this way
Can't stop the tears from falling down your face
There's always a problem with me
The anger just lingers all day and night
Where do you turn when you have no one
People say they'll be there but they're really not
Feeling alone just makes things worse
Never feeling your worth anyone's time
Who really makes time for you when you need someone
You really can only rely on yourself
Why does a crisis have to happen for someone to notice
There're signs of a crisis people just don't know them
Your insides are just crumbling away
You feel no one even cares
Will anyone show up and show they care
You say you care but do you really
It doesn't seem like it
I guess you have to remember
Even in the darkest of times
There is always light at the end of the tunnel

Being A Friend

Being a friend is a hard job
I will be what you need me to be
If you need me to care
I'll be there to care, I swear
If you need me to listen
I'll be there to carefully listen
I will always be the friend
The friend you want me to be

My Son Is Coming Home

I think about the day you came into this world
Oh, how much you have grown
You have grown into a charismatic young man
The day you joined the United States Air Force
In that moment, I was proud and sad all rolled up in one
The phone call that your deploying
I think of you everyday
My heart feels empty when we don't talk
Praying you and your squadrent will be safe
Hoping you'll come home safe and sound
Making it back to U.S. soil
Call me and say
I'm coming home, Mom
Watch out, I'm on my way

Little Moments

I adore all of our moments
Wish they would last forever
I adore when you hold me in your arms
Feelings that I get inside
You hold me tighter and tighter
Never do I want you to let me go
This love we feel together
I adore you and need you
More and more each day
The love we have for each other
I hope will forever stay

Which Door

As I walk down this road
That I have walked
Many times before
I feel like I'm walking through
The same door that I've walked through before
My life needs to change
I often wonder if rehab is that door
It hasn't worked before
Why now
I made the choice to walk through the rehab door
Now just waiting to see what's in store
This time is so different
I'm a new improved me
This time this door was the best choice for me

Shine Bright

Sometimes life leaves you feeling sad
Often sometimes even feeling mad
How does one cope
Knowing there is always hope
A smile from someone may pave the way
To bring you a brighter day
Hope is always there
Just you wait and see
Others will encourage you
Not to sit and stew
Shine as bright as you can
So everyone will see you glow
No time for negativity
Being positive is the way to go
You will see the sun shine through
Which can only benefit you

Another Chance

I thought it was special when we were together
I wish these moments could've lasted forever
You don't understand how I feel inside
My feelings for you just can't be denied
You seem to have forgotten all about me
I like you so much can't you see
I really want what we had back again
You seem to only want me as a friend
I want a friend, a best friend, and more
Can't you give me one more chance
Because maybe this friendship is really a romance

Friend ≠ Love

Did you ever love someone
And just know that they didn't love you
Did you ever feel like crying
To think what good will this do
Did you ever wonder where they are
And know they weren't with you
One moment you feel so excited
And the next you feel so blue
Don't ever fall in love my friend
You'll feel there's no satisfaction
Although it causes heartbreak
It happens everyday
When you do fall in love my friend
You hurt because your through
Believe me friend, you ought to know
Because I fell in love with you

Living in the Past

I find myself
Living in the past
Holding onto a love
That didn't last
Always dreaming of you
And the times that we've shared
Back when you once cared
But now your gone
And deep down I know
That maybe I should just
Let you go
I would if only
I could just find a way
To stop living in the past
And start living today

Into My Eyes

Oh, how I wish that you were here
That one person's voice I like to hear
The days have grown longer while we're apart
But you know that we were definitely meant right from the start
Even though you are so far away
I certainly will miss you everyday
You were my one true love
Sent from up above
Though you think there might be other guys
You'll always be the one
To look into my eyes

My Guy

Heavenly father full of grace
Please bless my baby's foxy face
Bless his hair full of curls
Keep him away from other girls
Give him hands so big and strong
But please have him keep them where they belong
Give him hands for you know why…
Bless him my Lord, because he's my Guy

Remember the Baby

Remember the fun we use to have
Troubles we had from being bad
Remember when we skipped school
And the lunch we shared that day
It was a bright sunny day
When we went to the barn and played in the hay
That day you asked me to be your girlfriend
I really thought we were ready
I remember our first fight
We actually made up that night
I recall the intense kissing that we shared
That night you said you would always care
I remember that precious day we went all the way
We couldn't forget because we have a baby on the way
Another day we went to the county fair
That was the day I knew you really didn't care
Because I went to the hospital in extreme pain
And you were nowhere to be found
I decided to keep the baby and Zoe is her name
However, the doctor said a few minutes ago
He said he was concerned about me but I really didn't know why
The doctor said he couldn't control the bleeding
I heard the doctor say he wasn't sure I was going to make it
All I cared about was that the baby was going to make it
There's no one here to help me through
I'm going to die what do I do
I tell you I love you, take care of the baby, and don't be blue

Liking Me

I never had the guts to say
I love you to your face
I know you don't know
I'm even around this place
You might even try to forget my face
I will never forget your warm embrace
I know you want to forget I care
So you can find someone else to be there
I will shed a tear or two
In fear of losing you
I wish we could start out slow
We could go at your pace
As time moves on
My love for you grows stronger
As time goes by
I will try not to cry
Someone is telling me lies
Why does everyone seem to like you
But I'm the one who really wants you
I always will I swear I do
I hope someday soon
You will like me too

I'd Ask for You

You have become the air I breathe
The air which sustains me
Thoughts of you in my head
Your laughter that entertains me
There's only one thing I want
And all I want is you
It is rather simple
And I will say it plain and true
You are the only person for me
It's simple but oh so true
If someone asked me for anything
I'd only ask for you

Need Me

Shall you ever need me for friendly advice
I will definitely be there to give it
Do you need me to send you love
I will be there to send it
If you need me to take a chance
I will be there to take it with you
If you ever need a smile
I will take a frown and break it
If you ever need some room
Your space is for taken
If you need me to be a friend
Friends are what we can be
If you maybe want to be with me
My hands are always here for the taken

Lonely Times

Lonely times aren't alone
When there's someone to make that loneliness grow
Lonely times are dreams that plummet
When people don't care and crash
Lonely times are love affairs
That break up because someone found out
Lonely times are mainly small
Seldom do people care at all
Lonely times sometimes wished
Are lonely times that are missed

Run to Me

Always run to me
Don't be afraid
You know I'll always be here for you
Always run to me
When your down and blue
Always run to me
When there is nowhere else to go
Come share your dreams with me
Don't be afraid
I will never let you down
Just you wait and see
See, if you can run to me in your time of need
Then we will know this relationship
Is one that was meant to be

Being Me

At times I may not be the person
That you really want me to be
In many ways I'm not the same
I once used to be
It might be hard for you at times
I'm growing up can't you see
It's not that I don't
Love you
I just need time
To be me

My Love, My Best Friend

Michael, you always seem to know
The right things to say and do
No matter where I am
I know I can count on you
There's never a problem
I can't tell you about
You give me support
And confidence without a doubt
I'm glad I have shared
My thoughts and feelings with you
You're my best friend Michael
I Love You

Died on Me

When I look in the big blue sky
All I could picture is his baby blue eyes
And when I look again
I just wanted to cry
I really couldn't believe
He really died
People told me
But I thought it was a lie
Now I'm living my life
Without him here
He'll always be in my heart
Until we meet again

Are You the One

You are the one
That God sent from up above
Full of joy
Always playful like a toy
Thinking of me frequently
Hopefully the one to be
I always want to say
I love you everyday
I know one day
You might possibly be gone
And someday someone else
May come along

More Than Friends

One day it started out as friendship
Which turned into something so much more
There is a love I feel for you
I have never felt for anyone before
You bring me so much happiness
When I'm feeling down
You end up joking around
I'm glad you can talk to me
About the stuff you do
But trusting me is what I'm glad you do
Because I definitely can trust you
You're my whole wide world
I need you to know
No matter what happens
I could never ever let you go

Golden Arrow

You remind me of a beautiful golden arrow
That is driven through my heart
Without you holding the arrow
It would tear me apart
I hope you realize
Just how much you mean to me
I love you to pieces
And I need you can't you see
If that arrow should ever break
It will forever tear my heart
Things would never be the same
It will forever be changed
I would be completely torn apart

Wish

While I will never regret
All the times we have been together
I will never forget how you cared so much
I really can't believe that it's over now
If I only had a four-leaf clover to wish upon
I would definitely wish to see you
For at least one more day

My Heart

I have a friend who is special to me
He means a lot
You surely can see
Seeing things for the better
When no one else does
V/e've been friends which seems like forever
Don't know how many years to be precise
He is so caring and kind
And always extremely nice
My hope is we never drift apart
Because he means so much to my heart

Still Loving You

It started out slowly
Grew day by day
The love for you inside me
The way I feel it will always stay
So many times I tried to tell you
But there are no words to say
And you found out anyway
Wow how much you mean to me
As playful as a dream
But the pain you put me through
You'll never really know
That my heart is slowly dying
Because my love is so strong for you
No matter what happens down the road
My love for you will forever grow

The Past of Addiction

Sometimes you find yourself
Holding onto a drug that you have
Knowing the drug doesn't always last
Dreaming of the next high
And that time you share together
You always think the addiction cares
But now you have nothing left
Deep down you know that
I hope this may be the final time
I just need to let it go
Now you need to find a way
To stop living in the past
And start living a new today

All I Want Is You

I'll tell you rather truthfully
Drugs and alcohol are the only thing I want
And all I want is more and more
I don't care if it is a bottle, needle, or a pill or two
You have been the very air I breathe
For so many years now
And the substance that has sustained me
It's all my thoughts tied up in one bad decision
And I know that it supposed to entertain me
It's only an hour or two
You're all that life has ever given me
This can't go on anymore
Now it's my rock bottom time
So I can get rid of you

Still Loving the Substance

It starts out slowly
And it grew day by day
Hour by hour
The love for a special substance
That never goes away
I have tried rehab and detox
But never could find the right day
Or the will power to stay anyway
Even though I never told anyone
They found out anyway
I've tried to make people see
That this substance means so much to me
But people never really understand or know
The pain the substance puts me through
My heart is slowly dying
Because my love for this substance
Is so strong and true
No matter what I decide to do with my life
After rehab and detox
My love for you is no more substance
And that's 100% totally true

Never Friends

Lonely times aren't alone
When your hanging out getting stoned
It's the love for a certain drug
And that drug never cares about you
Dreams that always crash
See special people that pass
Sometimes things seem so small
You often feel no one really cares at all
And feel your all alone
These drugs never were your friend at all

Drugs ≠ Friendship

There are no words to tell you
How much drugs mean to me
For years of friendship happy or sad
I thought I was grateful as can be
No work to go to
Only needles, bottles, and pills to share
The sunshine and shadows I see
Which drugs and alcohol often bare
For every trace of laughter
With my special drug or drink of choice
There are no words to tell you
How much you are not
A true friend to me

Drugs ≠ Heaven

I do believe God above created
Drugs and alcohol for me to love
He picks plenty of people out from the rest
He knew whatever it was I would love the drugs the best
My heart was definitely warm and true
Now it's gone from me to you
So, care for the drugs as I have done
Now you have two and I have none
When I get to heaven if you're not there
Should I wait for you by the big white stairs
If you're not there by a certain day
I'll know that you went to a different detox anyway
I'll give the angels back their wings
Maybe even their harps and everything
If I have to prove my love for you is true
I will go back to rehab and detox
Just for you

Control

If I had more will power
Drugs and alcohol
Would be out of my sight
I would stay at rehab and detox
And make a choice to do it right
I wish I could be normal in someway
There's nothing wrong with normal
Nobody's perfect
But control over myself is worth it someday

Rock Bottom

What does rock bottom look like
Rock bottom is knowing when to stop
Rock bottom is realizing how much is enough
Rock bottom is wanting to be free from addiction
Rock bottom is not always giving into temptation
Rock bottom maybe waiting for the right time
Rock bottom is realizing there is never a right time
Rock bottom seems so far away
Rock bottom can be a scary thing
Rock bottom may save you from yourself
Rock bottom may save you from everything
Especially from not coming back

Being Alone

Why does it always seem that I'm by myself
Sitting alone with no one home
I'm always waiting for someone to walk in the door
Whenever I'm at home I seem to be all alone
It's extremely sad when you find yourself alone
What am I going to do
How do I feel better
No one seems to understand how I feel
Is this feeling right or wrong
Can I feel this way
Without hurting someone's feelings
Does nobody want to stay
All I know is being alone is sometimes nice
Being alone doesn't have to be scary

Didn't Die

Do not stand at my grave and cry
I am not there
I do not sleep
I'm a thousand miles away
I am that sparkly diamond
That flashes in the snow at night
I am the gentle autumn rain
When you awaken in the morning
I am the swift rush of faith
I can be the soft star
That shines bright at night
Please don't stand at my grave and cry
My spirit is not there
My choice was to fly

Sending a Message

I send it off
It goes through snail mail
A stamp and envelope
Maybe even sealed with a kiss
It shuffles all around
Among all the other mail and packages
It contains an important message
That message is from me to you
To be treasured for you to see
It's a sweet little message to say "Hello"
With a big "I Love You"

Friendship

There are so many things we do each day
Some don't realize the great concern in the world
At times we do not stop and think about it at all
There're really important and nice things in life
The nicest thing is my friendship with you
Even if we don't have time to spend with each other
I want you to always know
How much I cherish you
And the friendship we have developed

Falling Autumn

As autumn flows in as a sign
As summer finally says good-bye
Say good-bye to hot summer days
and those beautiful summer nights
Those nights have come and gone
The cool autumn days are here to stay
As leaves start to turn different colors
We see beautiful green to gold leaves and yellow to red
There's a magical story that's about to be told
As fond memories from summer have past
Nature comes calling as autumn strolls in

What's Valentine's Day

Valentine's Day is pretty flowers
Valentine's Day is chocolate treats
Valentine's Day is cards and endearing words
All types of chocolatey sweets
This is the day for caring and sharing
This is the day for warm hugs and kisses
And "I Love You" with plenty of wishes

Dreams

My dream is to be free
Free from the feeling of anxiety
Free from sad and depressed
Free from negative family members
My dream is to be happy and completely free
Why is normal so hard to be
Do you have to be normal to be free
My dream is to just be me

Freedom

Freedom is the Air Force, Navy, Army, and Marines

Freedom is an all-around American Solider

Freedom is honoring The American Flag

Freedom is The Star-Spangled Banner

Freedom is air, land, and sea

Freedom is showing respect for the National Anthem

Freedom is our future

Freedom is being a proud American

Freedom is men and women doing their duty

Freedom is men and women who sacrifice for our country

Freedom ultimately doesn't come free

My Nana

Roses are red, violets are blue
I have a nana the best I can do
Her eyes are green,
Her heart full of gold
She's the one who brings me
in from the cold
her smile big from ear to ear
her love fills up the sky
Skin so soft and her heart full of love
She's definitely the one god sent from above
She's my best friend, my nana
For eternal time

My Nana Back

If I had my nana back
I wouldn't be out of her sight
Not for one day
I would stay with her until
The day she passed away…
I wish I was a normal kid
And could spend all my time with my nana
There's nothing wrong with that
But nobody's perfect
I guess

My Three Sons

You may not know how
Special you guys are to me
You're the best sons
That could ever be
We've been through good
And through bad
What a fun time together
Maybe now that your older and understanding
And I know your friends
I hope your trust in me
Never ends
All my life I hope you guys
Have looked up to me
I'm very proud of you all
And everything that you guys do
I've always taught you
So much along the way you know
I just wanted to tell you guys
How much I love you so

My Boo Bear

Memories trigger in my mind
Of how fun it used to be
A ten-month-old puppy that we brought home
When I was thirty years old
It isn't fair that in those years
I was gone from home to work
But he has gone from a crazy puppy
To old and weak in fourteen years you see
My one wish now would be
To stop the tumor from growing
and have him back to being free
But there's nothing more I can do now
Just wait and see he'll never be young
And peppy like before
The time that's left for him
Will hopefully be painless and fancy-free
For if love and hope
Were all he'd need
To have a healthy cure
My dreams would replace
His tumor
And make him healthy
Young and strong again
The Boo Bear who used to be

Nana

My nana was always there for me
Where ever I may go
She was always there to talk to me
I wanted her to know
Where ever I go or whatever I do
Nana there's no one
Who's more special than you

Letters from Michael

Strong feelings that form a bond
So many miles apart
But it doesn't mean the feelings are gone
Distance can be good sometimes
Because love seems to be always near
Deep down in my heart
There is nothing to fear
There is no way to describe
How much love I have inside
Flowing fast through me
Something I can't hide
Days go by I miss you
I miss you so much
Love reading your letters
It's my heart that you touch
Please love me like I love you
Together we can do anything
And make our dreams come true